I0487469

STOP!
Now Let's Go.

STOP!

Now Let's Go.
Formulas for Perpetual Wealth

MARVIN HUDSON

Outskirts Press, Inc.
Denver, Colorado

The opinions expressed in this manuscript are solely the opinions of the author and do not represent the opinions or thoughts of the publisher. The author has represented and warranted full ownership and/or legal right to publish all the materials in this book.

Stop! Now Let's Go.
Formulas For Perpetual Wealth
All Rights Reserved.
Copyright © 2009 Marvin Hudson
v3.0

Cover Photo © 2009 JupiterImages Corporation. All rights reserved - used with permission.

This book may not be reproduced, transmitted, or stored in whole or in part by any means, including graphic, electronic, or mechanical without the express written consent of the publisher except in the case of brief quotations embodied in critical articles and reviews.

Outskirts Press, Inc.
http://www.outskirtspress.com

ISBN: 978-1-4327-4109-9

Outskirts Press and the "OP" logo are trademarks belonging to Outskirts Press, Inc.

PRINTED IN THE UNITED STATES OF AMERICA

Acknowledgements

Throughout my life, there have been many people that have helped me become the person that I am today. So right off the top I would like to first give thanks to God who has given me all that I have asked for and more.

I want to say "Thank You" to the most important people in my life. They have always inspired me to do my best and to never settle for anything. To my parents: Marvin C. Hudson, Sr. and Sheila A. Hudson. Without them, I would not exist. Their love and support has propelled me to where I am today. I could not have had better parents. I would like to thank my sisters Veronica Cunnningham and Marva Hudson. They helped me stay on the right path. As a teen, the support I received from them kept me from going down a road that so many of my peers had the misfortune of traveling. Thanks Big Sisters! Thanks to my extended family: Aunts, uncles, cousins, nieces, and nephews. We have all been so close growing up. It seems as if I had more than 100 brothers and sisters. To my long time business associate and friend Deneen Rosendary. Everyone that is directly responsible for this book, I would like to say thank you. I have truly been blessed to have had so many great people help me with writing this book. I want to say "Thank You".

Introduction

I wrote this book as my way of giving back. Giving back is one of the greatest ways of showing thanks to God. Showing my gratitude for what God has done for me. Showing thanks and giving thanks ensures that I will continue to receive more blessings. I have been blessed and fortunate enough to have made millions of dollars. At this moment, I want to display my gratitude by showing others how they too can become wealthy.

I chose the title of this book in view of the fact that I felt many people were going about obtaining wealth in the wrong way. Or not even attempting to obtain wealth at all. Those that did make an attempt, found themselves hustling and bustling, aimlessly wondering around in circles; only to find themselves right back to where they started, or in a worse state. Many of us are spinning our tires as if stuck in the mud. Gaining no ground and expending way too much energy in the process. And now with less time than they had before they started. I feel that people need to stop what it is they were doing, and become skilled in a new way of thinking and doing.

In order to obtain wealth, you must stop behaving in a manner which does not create the results that you desire. Period! If the actions that you have been taking have not led you to accomplishing your life's goals; Stop! I felt obligated to write this book as a means to reach out and help someone that needed to be steered onto the correct course. If you happen to be on the wrong course, it does not matter how fast you are going. You will never get to your destination. Which are wealth, and the life that you want to live. We all have inside of us a desire to do bigger and better things. To have more and to do more. To live out our dreams. I will show you how to find the right road, and how to put your vehicle on cruise control and enjoy the ride.

No matter what the media says about the economy; nothing is more sound an investment than a good real estate deal. When I say "Good", I mean one which is profitable, and able to meet your goals. Whether the market is up or down, a good deal is a good deal. If you had the opportunity to buy a $1 million home for $5, would you let the media dictate to you and scare you out of buying that home? Absolutely not! You would probably give the seller $6 just to say thanks (Actually, I would probably offer them $4; always negotiate the best price). That is just an example of a good deal being a "good" deal no matter what the market is doing. Market conditions do affect real estate, but if and when you find a good deal, you can continue to profit. So do not allow the media, neighbors, relatives, and friends to talk you out real estate investing based on what they have heard on the news. Bottom line, a good deal is a good deal, no matter what.

When I got started in real estate investing, I was fortunate enough to have someone teach me the ins and outs to becoming a successful real estate investor. That success has helped me to live the life that I have always dreamed of. Starting other business ventures with the money that I have made, taking week long vacations whenever I feel like it, going to the beach whenever I feel like it, and making the time to go on field trips with my 10 year old son and his classmates. I could have never done those things when I had a job; a good Ole "9 to 5". Just as I have been taught, I now want to return the favor. That is why I included the words "Let's go" in the title. Because as you succeed, I succeed. I desire to help as many people as I can become millionaires just like me. We have a common interest; Your success = my success. Now let's get it.

By reading this book, you will find out why it is important for you to invest in real estate. You will understand the power that you have inside of you that will allow you to take flight, and become the person that you are and were always meant to be. You will learn techniques that if applied, will show you how to make more money than you have made in your entire life to this point. And in less time. You will discover why it is important for you to live out your dreams, and live up to your potential. This book is designed to set a spark underneath you to get you to take action, and begin to live, NOW! I will introduce to you a system which you can apply and make practical. A system which is thoroughly explained and easy to comprehend. I have found out that the simplest way of doing things, most often times, is the best way of doing things.

This book was made to inspire, motivate, and educate.

Any financial information that you may require should be received from your financial planner or your attorney. You are about to receive an education in real estate investing. I am sure that financial professionals will agree that real estate investing can make you a wealthy person. Are you ready?

"Failure is the opportunity to begin again more intelligently"
-Henry Ford

CHAPTER 1

Me

I was born and raised in Cleveland, Ohio, as the youngest of three children by Sheila and Marvin Sr. We lived in a public housing complex (The Projects). We had a typical, two bedroom apartment, in an area, like most big city public housing complexes, was full of the worst things that you could think of; Poverty, crime, drugs, prostitution, and hopelessness. My household was rare in the fact that I had a two parent household. Not many of my childhood friends had fathers living in their home. Not many of them had fathers in their lives period. During this time, I saw and experienced things that people would not find appropriate for a child to be exposed to. By the age of 8, I watched a man die right in front of me. The medical rescue team had arrived way too late to save him. He had been shot several times in the torso and midsection. I can remember the paramedics cutting open his clothing to expose his wounds. What a sight to see at 8 years old.

Hearing gun shots and seeing fights was not out of the ordinary. But for some reason, I always felt inside of me that what was going on around me was not right, and that

STOP! NOW LET'S GO.

I had a purpose. Something inside of me would not allow me to conform to my conditions. I had vision within me that allowed me to escape the hopelessness. Escape the despair. Break away from the madness.

I loved watching television shows. And my preferred television show was "Different Strokes." I appreciated how Arnold and Willis were taken in by a rich man and allowed to live in luxury on 5th Avenue in New York. "That must be the life," I would often tell myself. But for me, it was just the opposite; No elevator up to the Penthouse, just five flights of darkened, urine smelling stairs to get to the third floor of 5211 Outhwaite Ave.

From what I know now, we were not doing as well as I thought we were doing back then. Seeing through a child's eyes, I could only believe that things were going good. Not Different Strokes good, but okay. I always got stuff for Christmas. Birthdays brought about more gifts. And I was able to go to amusement parks and enjoy things that more privileged kids were taking advantage of. From my point of view at that time, we were living it up. As an adult, I now know that things were not as great as I thought they were. The violence, hopelessness, and desolation were all around. Drug dealers, drug abusers, pimps, prostitutes, and guns. That was my reality. How anything positive could be created in an environment which bred negativity.

My parents separated when I was 10 years old. I lived with my dad in the old apartment. My older sisters were old enough to be out on their own by this point. After two years, I went to live with my mom at my aunt's house. It was not far from where I grew up and it was also in public housing. For many months I would go back and forth from my aunt's house to my cousin's house. I would say, for about two years, I was homeless. I did not really feel comfortable in the situation I was in. At the age of 14, what is a child to do? My mom was working and she had a boyfriend that she spent a lot of time with. And my dad was now a single man, living and doing what single men do. I definitely did not fit into either of those equations.

Now through all this time, I was enrolled in school, right? And expected to succeed, right? Well around the time of my parents' separation, I was placed in honors classes, called Major Work at that time. I was placed in class with other intelligent students, and kept separated from the general population. The ones that were not expected to make too much of themselves. I guess the school system felt that it would be best to keep the gifted students away from the "riff raff."

School work was always easy for me. I did not like school, but the work was not difficult. I would get disciplinary action taken against me quite often because I was a class clown, Literally! It was not a good day for me unless I did or said something funny. At least I thought my stunts and antics were hilarious. One example of this occurred on the second day of my being in the honors classes. A girl seated next to me returned to her seat. As she began to sit down, I pulled her chair out from under her. She hit the floor. I was laughing hysterically. I looked around only to see that I was the only one that found humor in this gag. That gag had played well in the regular classes, not in Honors Class. I am sure the elementary school teachers thought my parents were doing a horrible job with me at home, but that was not the case. In school I completed all of my work. Got straight "A" reports cards, but my clown-like attitude brought bad marks to my conduct and behavior grades. I was smart; I just would not "act" right. See how schools train us to be conformists?

I enjoyed the summers when I played little league football. My family and I always thought that I would play in the NFL. When I got to Jr. High School, my mom and I finally found an apartment in the same neighborhood but in a different public housing complex. I finally had my own room. I continued to play sports with hopes of making it to the NFL. As I got older, I began dating, and eventually met the mother of my children. I was 14 years old at the time, and we were seeing a lot of each other. My mom was never home and her mom was out as well. That left us a lot of time to get to know each other. About a year later, at the age of 15, I was a father. I remember the time when I found out that my girlfriend was pregnant. I arrived home from football practice. Opened the door and to my surprise, I see her mom, my sister, my mom, and my girlfriend. Out of nowhere my sister laughs and says, "You about to be a daddy!" If ever there was a time to make a wish and disappear, that was the time. I should have been listening during Health class when they said that it only took one time to make a baby.

My mom asked, "Why didn't we use any protection?" I was thinking, "It's a little too late for that question." I was silent. I did not know what to do or say. It was definitely not how I envisioned finding out I was going to be a dad. Instead of feeling overjoyed and happy, I thought, "noooooo, not me, how could this have happened?" But it was clear how it happened. Leave unsupervised a teenage boy and girl, going through puberty, and guess what you get? A baby.

So now, I am a teenage father. I knew in my mind at

that point that I was not going to be a statistic. I was definitely not going to be caught in the cycle of poverty despite what was actually appeared on the surface. I knew many teenage fathers. Many of them were high school dropouts, or never even went to school at all. The men that I knew that had become fathers at an early age were all men that had to immediately begin to take care of a family. So, they dropped out of school to get jobs or to earn money to take care of their children. A father at 15. Living in public housing. Things were not looking promising. But I knew inside of me then, the type of life I wanted to live. So, I continued to play football in high school and gained the attention of a few small schools. I felt that if I made it to the NFL, I could make enough money to support my family. I applied to several colleges and had taken the college admissions tests. The scores that I received were good enough to get me into college and be eligible to play football. Now I am on my way.

One incident which occurred during my senior year in high school involved a meeting with the Senior Guidance Counselor. I still remember his name to this day. I will never forget it. I can credit some of my success to him. Even though he saw no potential in me. During the meeting that I had with Mr. Guidance Counselor, we were discussing my plans after graduation. I mentioned that I had planned to attend college. Mr. Guidance Counselor felt that it would be better for me to attend auto-mechanics school or a trade school. "What! You mean to tell me that after all of these years in Honors Classes, I still do not have a chance to go to college?"

I was thinking, "this guy must be drunk, or just stupid." I knew for a fact that I am going to college. Now thinking back on that event, I wonder how many Misguidance Counselors (which should be there official title; they offer little guidance and limited counseling) have directed students to not follow their dreams. Or reach higher. There was not a doubt in my mind that I was going to attend college. That meeting set a flame beneath me that has kept me driven for years. All through college, when things got rough, I would always think back to that meeting that I had in high school. I used that as motivation to get me over and above the obstacles that I faced. I had to prove to the Misguidance Counselor that he was mistaken.

Two months after being told that I ought to attend auto-mechanics school, I was accepted into Ohio Northern University, Ada, Ohio. Three months later, in June, I became the first in my family to graduate from high school. Five years after that, I became the first in my family to graduate from college. I had earned a Bachelor of Arts in Criminal Justice. All of that accomplished by a kid that, according to the high school Misguidance Counselor, should have gone to auto-tech school. Not saying that anything is wrong with being an auto mechanic, but it was just not for me. I did not know a steering wheel from a muffler. I had never had any desire to be a mechanic.

I feel that schools set us up to be employees. It is a 12 year process. Worker bees. We all have fallen for it. I did not even know what was going on. I bet you did not know either. We are indoctrinated into Operation "Get A Job" at age 5 when we start kindergarten. "Go to school, work hard, and one day you will get a good job!" Do you ever remember hearing that? Why weren't we taught how to create a job from doing what we truly loved? Why did they not teach us how to do what we loved? Why were we not taught how to be the Boss?

After graduating from college, I returned to my old neighborhood. My mom had moved out of the apartment, that we previously shared, and into the suburbs. Now I have my own place, I have a job, and I am on my way to that 3 bedroom, 2.5 baths that I had been dreaming about. The only thing standing in my way was a Job. I had a county job. Anyone that knows anything about county jobs, know that you are not going to get rich working in the public sector. And being rich is what I had hoped to be upon finishing college. I had done what I was misled into believing: Graduate from high school, graduate from college, and watch the dollars start to flow your way. That was not the case. I was earning $30,000 a year, minus student loan payments, minus child support (oh yeah, we had another child, that makes two, but our relationship did not last=child support). I was bringing home almost no money. Only enough money to pay my rent and eat. When you don't have enough money, eating can sometimes become optional. I failed to figure in all the expenses of living, and was forced to look for a second job. I worked very hard. Too hard if you asked me. I had a second job, but that only left me with chasing my tail; around and around getting nowhere but dizzy. It had to be a better way than this. There has got to be.

To lessen my expenses, I moved out of my apartment and into a home with my cousin. It was not the most comfortable of environments. But I had to do what I had to do. I started thinking about what I could do to get enough money to be able to afford my own place. I remembered an associate telling me how his dad had made money investing in real estate. "Bingo!" I thought. That is what I will do. But how? I have over $25,000 in student loans, credit card debt from cards that I abused while in college (thanks a lot Visa and MasterCard), and I do not have any money saved up for any type of investing. Many sleepless nights went by, as I pondered my escape out of my miserable debt and my despondent existence.

I was up late one night watching television. I saw a commercial about a real estate program that you could buy for $200, and it would show you how to buy homes, and make money with "NO MONEY DOWN!" I remembered thinking that this guy on this commercial has been coming on ever since I was a kid. It must be something to this. So I bought the program. It set me back over $200, but I figured it was a small investment to make to earn Thousands.

So now I have the discs and the book from the real estate program. I am very motivated to make some money now, and this is going to help me get started. I was hoping that as soon as I started the program I would be making money. After a year of studying and reading, reading and studying; Nothing. Not a house, not even an outhouse was bought. I packed up the program and thought that maybe I should just get a second job and pay off some bills, and just get by that way. I had that "just defeated, I want to quit" attitude for about a year.

I was working two jobs now. Over 60 hours a week now. I felt as if I was working myself to death. Therefore, I decided that I needed a vacation. So I got on the Internet, and booked myself a trip. I could not afford an island resort. I had to settle for the next best thing; Atlanta, Georgia.

I had relatives there, and I also considered moving there, so Atlanta here I come. One day, while vacationing in Atlanta, my niece introduced me to her friend. He was a few years younger than me. She introduced me as being a real estate investor. I am thinking "Oh boy, I hope he does not ask for any help, I have not invested in anything but the real estate program." From the looks of it, he was not doing too badly, as he had a brand new BMW 745 sitting in the parking lot. He happened to be a real estate investor, for real.

Later that night, he and I went to have some beverages at a local club. We were riding in his car. He was asking me questions about the market and what I have done in my area. You know: things that professional real estate investors talk about. I told him that I had just gotten started, and what my plans were. After listening to me ramble on clueless, he told me that I was going about things the wrong way. And that I needed to do things his way. Of course my ears and eyes were wide open now. I am ready to learn as much as I could. Especially from a guy that had bought and sold over 100 homes. He explained to me the way he does real estate deals. His way of doing things was nothing like the way that I was going to approach it. He went into detail about how deals are done, and how he had made money in real estate. He also explained the process. As we spoke, he had a commercial real estate (office buildings, multi-family, strip malls, land) deal pending. He stood to make over $500,000 on that deal. He explained to me that the same rules apply. He strongly suggested that I use his formula for success. After he was done coaching me, I can remember sitting in the BMW passenger seat simmering with the anticipation of what I was going to do as soon as I returned home.

Needless to say, I stayed in contact with my new best friend from Atlanta. He walked me through my first two deals, in which I made $10,000 and $25,000 in three months. Without spending a dime of my own money. My first deal was a two family home which rented for $1150 per month. I bought the house for $85,000 and received $10,000 at the closing of the deal. I also collected the rent of $1150 and put that in my pocket, as the first mortgage payment was not due for another 45 days. Within the next year, I would purchase eight more homes and pocketed $55,000. Great! Do you think I am ready to quit my job? Absolutely! But, an amazing and unforeseen issue arose. Who was supposed to manage these properties? I certainly was not qualified. I did not know a screwdriver from a hammer. Some of my former tenants will testify to that.

Now, at that point, I owned ten properties. As with many things, problems do occur. Sinks needing fixed, furnaces, hot water tanks, toilets needing fixed, fights needing to be broken up between tenants (yes, it happens), and vacancies. I failed to take into account the maintenance and upkeep that was involved with having investment property. And of course I did not ask my experienced real estate friend about this part (Mistake!). I had to learn about property management the very hard way.

Instead of hiring trained, licensed, and experienced professionals, I decided that fixing stuff could not be that difficult. "I could just do it myself." Wrong! Boy was I wrong! I have been electrocuted, burned with torches, soaked from leaking pipes, attacked by dogs, and trapped underneath a bath tub(really!), all because I attempted to manage the properties myself. Big mistake!

After two years of mismanaging my properties, I was

ready to sell each and every one of them. I did not want to be a landlord anymore. I had had enough of the late night calls, the neighbors' complaints, and the city councilman. "Who wants a house?" I was more than willing to sell the homes for exactly what I owed on them, just to get them off of my hands. I was a very motivated seller. But there were no takers. What was I going to do? The money that I had made from these deals was disappearing as I had to keep feeding money into these homes. The price that I was asking was too high. I was trapped; stuck with homes that no one wanted to buy and no one was currently occupying. I had no escape plan or exit strategy. I was forced into foreclosure. I had no way to pay the mortgages on ten homes. The lowest point in my life. Having to watch my homes being auctioned off at a sheriff's sale. After that, I had to file for bankruptcy. I had no money and I had no income. A sad, sad, sad time.

After that stage in my life, in no way did I give up on my dreams of being a successful real estate investor. I learned many, many lessons from my failed attempt at being a landlord/property manager/referee/pest controller. Lessons that could not have been learned at a seminar, class, or university. Life Lessons. I knew that the only way to live the lifestyle that I wanted to live was by investing in real estate, again. But this time, doing it the right way. My way. The way that I will teach you later in this book.

If you are motivated and ready to get some serious wealth in your life, and live the life that you feel you were destined to have; If you feel that you have the ability to follow instructions, are motivated, and ready to put lessons into action; then follow my instructions, and you will be able to learn from my mistakes. You will also learn from my many, many successes. The failures that I experienced have been priceless with regards to the lessons that I learned. I would not trade that experience for anything in the world.

After having lost everything in foreclosure and bankruptcy, and being broke. I have since bought and sold over Three million dollars in real estate (that's $3,000,000). Not bad for a teenage father on welfare, that was told to give up on his dreams, after facing homelessness while living in public housing, and having filed bankruptcy. I had no formal training, no privileged upbringing, no inheritance, and not even a rich uncle to borrow from. And if I could do it, guess who else can? _____! (Fill in the blank)

How did I do it? How was I able to bounce back? At the lowest point in my life I improved my relationship with God. It is funny how even the most self-centered person always seems to find their higher power when things are not going well. It is no coincidence. That is how we are designed. To connect with our Higher Power when we need answers; when we need solutions. Every single morning when I would wake up, I asked God to help me be strong and stay focused. I thanked him for the things that I have had, the things that I have now, and the things that I will have. Now, I am not going to dwell into religion or religious philosophies of any kind. I am not trying to place my beliefs on you or your Higher Power. I am just explaining that in order for you to be successful at anything you have to do these three things:

God first in all things.
Tithe or donate to charities
Give thanks, daily

Now some of you may be asking: How do you tithe or donate to charity when you don't have any money at all? And that is a good question. The answer to that question is addressed later in this book in the chapter entitled: Giving Back. A smile, holding open a door for someone, or doing a good deed or gesture, are ways of giving that do not require money. Do not ignore homeless persons or panhandlers when they approach you for some "spare change." I have learned that by just acknowledging a homeless person that asks you for money is sometimes more valuable to them than money. Just by telling them "sorry I do not have it", instead of ignoring them, could at least give them validation that they exist. Sometimes realizing that you do exist is all that we need to get us back on track.

Now are you ready? I have done it. Am I better than you? No. Am I smarter than you? No. Then what are you waiting for? It is time for us to begin our journey together. For the time that it takes for you to read this book, and sometime after you complete it, we will have a connection. You are analyzing words and ideas that are originating from my mind and heart. I am communicating with you even though I cannot see you nor you me. The next chapters will enlighten you and educate you on how you can begin to STOP running in place and chasing your tail in a circle, and go get the life that you want. STOP! NOW LET'S GO!

"You have to expect things of yourself
before you can do them"
-Michael Jordan

CHAPTER 2

Just Over Broke or J.O.B. for Short

Many of you that are reading this are probably in a situation where you want to better yourself or better your way of life. For most of us, that better way of life involves having money. Money is NOT the root of all evil. Selfishness is the root of all evil. Some of you that are reading this book are employed, maybe one or two jobs. When we were children, who amongst us had imagined that they would one day have to work two jobs? I know I did not. I am sure most of you did not fathom that as well. Who wants to work 50, 60, or 70 hours a week? Doing something that you hate doing. And at the end of the month, what do we have to show for our hard work? More bills, more bill collectors, and more of having the same of what you had last month: not much. I was there. I can remember working two jobs. From the time I would wake up in the morning, to the time I would commute home from the second job, would allow me just enough time to get in 6 hours of sleep so that I could rest up and do it all again. I did not remember signing up for that life. It just seemed to have happened. On the other hand, my bosses, and supervisors did not appear to be having this problem. They were making enough money from running the company or business, that it was unnecessary for them to have to work more than one job. The "dead end" position that I held in the company or business did not allow me the opportunity to say "one day, I am going to work my way up to the top at this place." There was no promotion. A dead end job in every sense.

If you happened to have made it through the American School System like myself, congratulations. We have been bamboozled, led astray, hood winked. We were told for twelve straight years that if we worked hard enough in school, that one day we would be able to get a "good job." Does that sound familiar to anyone? I can remember hearing it like it was yesterday. We were bombarded with this myth that having a "job" would give you the "American Dream". A house, backyard, two car garage, and maybe a swimming. We have been set up to think like employees from day one. I have come to the realization that Employees do not make the money in a company. The woman or man that owns the company makes all the money, and spends little or no time doing any work. All of the work is done by the employees. It has been estimated that 95% of the American population make 5% of the money. While 5% of the American population make 95% of the money. If you are an employee and you work for someone else, you already know which group you are in. So what does that tell you? Maybe you should try becoming the boss. Get into that 5% group.

Now I am very much for education. In America we have the privilege of free education. And if you have kids,

I encourage you to positively support and encourage your kids to get the best education that you as parents can afford. But most schools have helped extinguish our hopes for wealth, and has not nurtured our natural born entrepreneurial spirit. How did we all get caught in these jobs that do not allow us to live the life that we envisioned when we were kids?

The type of job and how much money you make, determines the majority of the aspects and details of your life. Your job dictates what type of home you will live in and the type of car you will drive, if any at all. Your job dictates to you how many children you will have, the types of clothes you will wear, and the type of foods you will eat. Where you vacation will also be dependent upon what type of job you have as well. Some of the most beautiful buildings and monuments have been built in some of the most exotic of locations around the World. Many things like the Pyramids of Egypt, The Great Wall of China, and The Eiffel Tower are spread around the globe. They are not in America. They are not in your backyard. How are you supposed to be able to see and experience these things when you have no money? Why should only a privileged few get to see and experience the 7 wonders of the World? Why not you? Those things were scattered about the earth for you to go to them and see what wonders Earth holds. How could you afford to do that? With your current income, how many checks would you have to save up to take your family and yourself on a vacation to Europe or Africa?

Money determines what type of life you will live, If you like doing things such as spending time with your children or going to visit and spend time with an elderly relative, your job will let you know if you are free to do those things. Your job will also dictate how much you can give to charity or to someone less fortunate. Having a job that does not pay much has led to some people feeling as if the best charity is right in their own home. One of the best days of my life was attending a field trip with my 10 year old son and his classmates. We went to a farm/petting zoo in Ohio. It was a great time, and one that I will never forget. If I were still working at my job, I may have missed out on that event had my employer told me I could not get the day off. The only thing I could have said to my son was "sorry, maybe next year." Has this ever happened to you? Next year will come, and if you are in the same job, you would still have to ask for permission from your employer to spend time with your children.

Many people have grown content with the false sense of comfort and security that a job brings. Especially one with "good benefits." Many people feel as if they have made it if they can get a job with good benefits. But how safe is it to have a comfortable job? If you are looking for comfort, how comfortable could you be knowing that your job could be gone at any time? Everyday scores of Americans are losing their jobs to layoffs, plant closings, and outsourcing. Now what are you supposed to do when you have a mortgage, car payments, and little Billy has just started college, and the company tells you that they are closing in a few months? It is unsafe and unwise to balance your life on the assumption that your job will be there forever. Depending on your job and relying solely on your pay check for the next thirty to forty years is unsafe, unwise, and will not get you the life that you really want.

Some of the most precious moments in your life can

be missed or go unnoticed due to the fact that your job will not allow you the time or money to enjoy life to the fullest. It is a for certain that no one knows when their last day on this Earth will be. Don't you think it is time to start living the life that you want to live, Today? Instead of day dreaming and fantasizing about tomorrow; Start taking action, and creating your tomorrow. Do not leave it to chance. Tomorrow is going to come, and when it comes, will you still be punching the clock? Staying in your lane in the Rat Race? Rushing out of the house in the morning to join the other half of the city on the freeway, all at the same on ramp, all at the same time. Rush Hour!? Who's bright idea was this? I like to think of the Rat Race as a relay race. Many of you are running in the Rat Race, and without knowing, subconsciously passing the baton to your children. So that they too can do with their lives what they have seen you do all of your life. While the wealthy teach their children how to become the boss, not the employee.

I know some of you are in a position where you really love your job and doing whatever it is that you do for a living. That is great. If that happens to be your situation. And if so, continue working. I am not saying call your boss right now and tell him what he can do with his job. What I am saying is that you should love living for a living. And doing what you love to do. This book was written to give you more options. So that you can work at your job not because you have to, but because you want to. If you are not doing that which you love, you are not living.

We have determined that your job just will not get you the life that you want to live. You have to have money. Money is a beautiful thing. So much good can be done with money. You want abundance. And now is the time to get more. Abundant Life, Abundant Love, Abundant More! There is more to being alive than just living. And no better time than NOW to start living the life that you want.

"A hundred times every day I remind myself that my inner and outer life depend upon the labor of other men, living and dead, and that I must exert myself in order to give in the measure as I have received and am still receiving"
--Albert Einstein

CHAPTER 3

Alive

One day you were born. At that moment, you were 100% potential. You had the world in front of you, and in the palm of your hand. You were born with a brain that was able to calculate and learn at the speed of light. There are computers that are priced at thousands of dollars that cannot do what but a portion of your brain can do. Isn't that amazing? You were born an explorer and a discoverer. You had eyes, ears, a mouth, a nose, hands, and feet. You were also given this device called the Heart that has this strange mutual relationship with the Brain. At times, they work together, sometimes they do not. However, you were built to succeed in the world that you were born in to. You were not born with gills or fins, because you were not born to be underwater. You were not born with wings, because you were not born to fly through the air like a bird. Sans birth defects, you were born as a perfect human being. Able, ready, and capable of conquering any and all challenges headed your way.

You arrived here, on Earth, with everything that you

needed to be successful on this Planet Earth. You were born with all of the tools to succeed. There was nothing that you could not accomplish or achieve. Everything was possible. The sky was the limit. You had countless options available. Some of your parents even fantasized about your future career path: mom wanted a doctor, dad a football player. Someone successful you were going to be. And so, that being the case, how did you get to where you are now?

For many of us, as we got older, we began to act carefully. Too careful. By being careful, I mean we stopped wanting to take chances. Taking chances might take you out of your "comfort zone". And we all know how we love to be comfortable. Not wanting to take risks. But Great risks = great rewards. As adults, a good number of us are more concerned about the pain we would feel if we failed, rather than the experience we would gain if we tried and did not succeed. The older some of us get, the more "careful we get". Just think of some of the things that you did as a child, and how your behavior and actions began to get a little more safer and less risky as you got older. To the point now where you are thinking, "I cannot believe that I used to do that!" You took chances, you enjoyed your life, and you were happy. What happened to that person?

You were not put on Earth to fail. Your mission upon birth was for success. You have all the tools that you will ever need. Tools that were designed to help you to do or to be whatever it is that you want. You were born at exactly the right time when the world needed you. Have you let us down? Have you lived to your fullest potential? You have the greatest problem solver in the universe, right in between your ears: your brain. And imagine; you were born with it, it was free of charge. The only requirement of you was that you used and took care of it.

I have heard people often times say that no one is perfect. I have a different take on that subject. I feel that if you are truly yourself, you are being the perfect you. Yes you may not do things that are always perfect. And yes you may make mistakes from time to time. But we must be reminded that we are perfect. I am the perfect me and you are the perfect you. How could you not be? God makes no mistakes. Being the perfect you allows for mistakes and miscues to be taken with a grain of salt. Everyone is capable of perfection, if they are true to themselves. Be true to yourself by being the best you that you can be.

You have been given all of the tools that you will ever need. In the future, if any other tools are required, like a third lung to handle polluted air, your brain is designed to adapt to make your life easier. That is how we were designed. With the ability to adapt to any situation. Relatively speaking. you have been placed in the right environment to succeed, now. So why are you not living the life that you want to live?

With regards to lifestyle and happiness, the lack of money is the one circumstance which can limit both your lifestyle choices and your happiness. If you do not have money, how are you supposed to know what and who you really are? Without money, how do you discover the many talents and capabilities that you have? How are you so unsure that you are not meant to be the greatest pilot to ever take control of a plane, if you never have the resources to try? How do you know that you were not meant to discover a hidden treasure in the Caribbean Sea, if you never get enough money to go scuba diving? You have to be able to experience LIFE to the fullest. Money allows you to do so. When you have no money, you have a limited existence. Limited options, limited potential. Limited ability to serve.

Now many people have made the argument that money does not buy you happiness. That may or may not be true. It is a topic that is definitely arguable. What is undoubtedly true, and with no argument, is the fact that you cannot be happy and live the life that you want if you are broke. This is for certain.

So now what? You know that you want more. You know that you are not happy with your current life and your current finances. You know that your job is not providing you with the money to do the things that you really want to do with your life. You have all the tools to be successful. You have a brain that is more powerful than any computer ever made. So how do you get from where you are, to where you want to be? If you say that you want to live a better life, Make enough money to retire early, Spend more time with your children, Take longer vacations to farther away places, Eat at the finest restaurants, Donate to your favorite charity, Drive the fastest car, and wear the finest clothes, here is what you have to do: Invest in Real Estate. "But how do I do that? I can barely afford to put gas in my car" you ask.

If you are capable of reading and comprehending; grasping and applying; you are capable of making millions. Just like I did. All from nothing. All from perfecting a formula. All from investing in Real Estate.

"Be strong and of a good courage, fear not, nor be afraid…for the Lord thy God, goes with you; he will not fail you, nor forsake you."
-Deuteronomy 31:6

CHAPTER 4

How it is Done.

In America, 70% of all millionaires became so by investing in real estate. And many of them did not become millionaires until they began to invest in real estate. Many millionaires invest their money into real estate no matter their primary business. People are always going to need a home. Homes are going to be needed to accommodate the millions of people in this country, and the millions that will be coming to this country over the next few decades. Where will these new Americans live? Doesn't it seem as though there is no more room for them? And who are they going to rent from? Why not you?

Real estate is one of the best ways to establish wealth, build wealth, and protect your future. With real estate, you could set yourself up with deals that could result in the purchasing of buildings or homes. Property that could be passed down to your children and to your children's children. Real Estate investing has made more new millionaires than any other field. And it is always going to be that way. Even the millionaires that made their money during the dot.com boom of the 90s figured out that in order to keep their wealth, they had better invest in real estate.

Investing in real estate consists of the purchase and sale of:

Single family homes	Strips Malls
Duplexes	Land
Triplexes	Office Buildings
Multi-Unit	Malls
Apartment Buildings	

For our purposes here, we are going to concentrate on single family homes. However, with our formula, we can apply it to any type of real estate.

There has been recent news of how bad the market is, and how in today's economy, now is not a good time to buy real estate. DO NOT BELIEVE IT! There is never a bad time to take advantage of a good deal. In this country, the economy is cyclical. Things that have happened in the past will happen in the future. It is a cycle. Things go from bad to worse and back to bad. But for the most part, good. Property values have increased since the beginning of the 20th century. SO why would you pass up on the opportunity to buy a home for $1 just because the news said that the market was bad? A deal is a deal. I will show you how to recognize a good deal and how to take advantage of a good deal. Sometimes all it takes is one great deal to create a snow ball effect. Next thing you know, you are rolling in the dough. Unstoppable.

Many of you that have not invested in real estate before or have no knowledge of home financing, may be under the belief that you have to have a lot of money in the bank(or in your mattress). Also, many believe that you have to have perfect credit to be a successful real estate investor. Yes, having a lot of money to start is nice; and great credit will help. But it is not necessary. The things that you need as a beginning investor is knowledge (how to find a good deal), technique(how to acquire a good deal), and attitude (how to carry yourself as a professional real estate investor). Once you have a system or formula that works, you keep applying it. Over and over and over again.

The more you know, the more you grow.

To start on your road as a real estate investor, you have to know how to find and recognize a good deal. A good deal is defined as being one where you are confident that you can achieve your goal with the deal. Your goals may include buying and quickly selling (Flipping), or buying and holding the property. There are a number of ways to find deals. You can look in the classified section of newspapers, websites, and driving in a neighborhood, any neighborhood. Maybe you grew up in a neighborhood and you are comfortable there. If you find a neighborhood that you are not comfortable with, remember this lesson: Just because you would not live there does not mean that someone else would not. I cannot recall how many deals I may have missed out on when I first started, by only looking in areas of town that I felt were right for me to live in. And making my decision base solely on whether or not I would live there. Remember, if you are going to have investment rental property, your primary goal is to have it occupied with a good paying tenant. And have the tenant pay you an income and/or pay the house off for you. A good property management company can help you with any and all of your rental and tenant concerns. Property management will be covered later.

Being able to recognize deals will come with experience. After you begin to see them, you will start to see more of them everywhere. It's like when you got your new car, you did not see as many people driving them until you got yours, right! (Think about it) You begin to have an eye for it.

You will start to recognize and say, "hey, that looks like a great deal." Many deals will come to you as you establish yourself as a professional real estate investor. Relatives, coworkers and former coworkers will begin to bring you information on available properties as they become available. That's why you want to start off by telling everyone that you are a professional real estate investor. And mean it! Even if you have not bought a thing. Tell everyone that you are a professional Real Estate Investor.

When you are looking for deals, be it in the newspaper or a website, try to get an idea of what the houses in that area are worth. This can be done by searching that city's or county's website, or asking your local Realtor. If you see "For Sale" signs in yards, engage the sellers or call the number that is listed on the sign. Ask them what is the price of their home. This is an inexpensive way to check the market. Try Finding the asking price of numerous homes in a particular neighborhood. Again, this helps you gauge the market.

Once you find out what the house is worth, then you can begin to calculate your offer along with your next moves. Make offers, make offers, make offers. Only after the seller tells you what they are asking for the property. You will want to kick yourself if you offer someone $50000 for a house and later find out that they would have taken $35000. Your first offer may not be accepted by the seller. Your second offer may be rejected by another seller. But sooner or later, you are going to get a "Yes". It's like fishing, the more you throw out your line, the better your chances of catching fish.

Let us look at an example of a good real estate deal. Say that I found a house at 123 Main Street for $45000. I am familiar with that neighborhood and I know that all of the homes in that neighborhood, specifically on that street, are worth at least $80,000. I might be interested in checking this house out. Thus far, the numbers are looking good. It appears that this home has about $35000 in equity($80000 value - $ 45000 sale price). Just from looking at the numbers, and not having seen the house, I would say that this one definitely deserves my attention. Now, the home is being sold by an elderly couple that is ready to get out of town. They are retired and ready to move to warmer climate. I found that information out during the call that I made to them.

You will find that when you call the motivated sellers and you are professional and courteous, they will tell you everything that you want to know. Information is King. Here is how the call may go:

Me: Hello, My name is Marvin, I am a real estate investor and I am interested in purchasing your home. I see in the ad that you want $45000 for it. Could you give me more information on it.

Seller: Yeah, we are ready to sell, we are trying to move to Florida before the winter gets here. It's 3 bedrooms, 1 bath. We've been trying to sell it for two months now.

Me: If you don't mind my asking, how much do you owe on the home?

Seller: The home is paid off. We don't have a mortgage. We are basically giving it away to sell it quicker.

Me: What are you planning on doing with all that money when you get to Florida?

Seller: The money is going in the bank. We'll just lay up on the beach and go fishing. My wife and I love to fish. We have another home in Florida that we are going to move into.

Now I have been able to get some important info from this seller. One, he is a motivated seller (someone that is ready and very eager to sell). Two, he does not have a mortgage on the home (Free and Clear). Three, he does not have a pressing need to have all of his money right away. He is just going to put it in the bank.

After getting the information from the seller, I ask to come over to the house to make an offer. I go to the house to take a look around. With a price like that, the home could have needed $10000 in repairs and it would have still been a good deal. I am not planning on using any bank financing with this deal. What I proposed to the seller is this: I purchase the house with owner financing. The seller acts as the bank. Owner financing allows me to sign a contract/purchase agreement to buy the house for a specified price. Then, I pay the seller a monthly payment for a certain number of years. I promote the monthly payments to the seller as monthly income to him. That way it sounds good to him and he will then become more comfortable with the offer. I will agree to pay him $400 dollars over the next 36 months. The payments that I make to the seller will go towards my down payment. I will assume all the duties as property owner (taxes, utilities, insurance) and get all tax advantages of being a home owner. The seller will be able to relax in Florida, collect $400 a month for 36 months, with the full amount due after 36 months. I contacted A property management company. The property management company explained to me every service that they are able to provide, if I hire them. They have informed me that I can rent the home out for around $800 per month. So here is the wrap up. The seller has agreed to accept $400 over 36 months, that is a total of $14400. I will owe $30600 after 36 months. If I don't pay the seller, he could just foreclose on the property and attempt to sell it again.

I get the home cleaned up. An inspection was done prior to the signing of the deal. The home did not require any major work, just cosmetics. I hire a property management company to find and place a tenant in the home, and charge the tenant $800 per month. The tenants payments of $800 covers the $400 owed to the seller, $12 for property management (fee is usually 3% of collected rent), and other fees amount to around $100 per month. The tenant will pay the utilities(electric, gas, water). That leaves me to pocket over $250 each month. At the close of this deal, the only thing I had to pay for out of pocket was the filing of the purchase agreement with a title company. This was done to protect myself and the seller. And I get that money back when the new tenant pays their first month's rent and deposit. My credit was not checked. No loan application. NO income verification was needed. I did not need to qualify for a bank loan. Win-Win-Win! Everyone is happy. Now what do I do when the 36 months are up? Where do I get $30600?

The 36th month is fast approaching. I have been collecting rent on this property for the past 35 months and pocketed over $8000. I have a stake in this home for $14400 as I have given the seller $400 for the past 36 months. I now have to come up with $30600. I have a lease option on a $80000 home, (assuming the property value did not go up or down over the past 36 months) that I owe $30600 on. Do you think It will be hard for me to get a loan on this home from a bank? Not at all. The bank will see that I have a down payment of $14400, therefore, I have a vested interest in the home. I am not too much of a risk. The bank feels that since I have $14400 into the property, I am not willing to take a lost by not paying back the home loan. Regardless of my credit, there will be a bank that will give you a loan for $30600 on a home that is worth $80000; especially since you have already made a down payment of $14400. Banks love deals like this. Even if you defaulted the loan, the bank should not have much of a problem reselling the home in the event of a foreclosure. Therefore, the bank is willing to take the risk. I get the loan for $30600, now the seller is paid off.

Now I make my monthly payments to the bank. My monthly payments to the bank at 8%(which is high, used as an example for a 30 year loan) would be around $200. You make payments to the bank for about a year. The $800 in rent that I receive from the tenant will cover that and leave the rest for me to pocket.

After a year. I decide that I want to refinance my home. So I go to a <u>mortgage broker </u>that specializes in getting loans for real estate investors. I refinance the house at $52000, so that I can take some of the equity out of the home and put it in my pocket(some banks will offer a equity line of credit). I pay off the $30600 from the first loan and pocket $21400 ($52000-30600). Now after just four years. I have in my pocket $21400 from a deal that I was already collecting and pocketing money from rents for the past four years. All of this with no money down, no initial credit approval or any bank to get me started. Take a minute to think about this. I suggest that you read it again.

Please note: The figures used in the example were rounded and excluded transaction and closing fees. They were excluded to better illustrate the example. Closing fees vary, but they are not that expensive. Also, you can have the costs associated with closing, rolled into the mortgage, which means that it is no money out of your pocket. The tenant will pay it back.

As a side note, this deal could have easily been refinanced sooner than four years. I wanted to illustrate to you the nuts and bolts of the process and how the formula, if applied correctly, can work. And how things work when you use your mind. I dealt with no tenants, never even met them. I collected no rent and I fixed no leaky toilets. I let the property management company do all that for me. Most property management companies will do whatever you pay them to do. From hiring repair people, to locating tenants, to evicting tenants, to cutting the grass. While they are doing that, all you have to do is walk to the mailbox every month to get your checks. Pretty nice, right?

Deals similar to the one in the example are all around you. You just have to be tenacious in your search. Apply your formula, Apply your formula, Apply your formula! I always say the active bird gets the worm. You can be early as you want, but unless you know how to act on a deal, it may just wiggle right out of your grasp.

That was a no money down approach to buying real estate and making money, fast. If you could do two or three deals like that a month, imagine how much money you could make. Pause for a minute and think about the monthly income that you would need in order to live the life that you want. The number of deals that you need to close each month will be determined by how wealthy you desire to become.

"Act boldly and unseen forces will come to your aid"
-Dorothea Brande

CHAPTER 5

Rehabs; Fixer Uppers

You have been doing deals like the example in the last chapter for some time now. You are getting the real estate investors' eye, and can now smell a deal a mile away. Now you want some big cash and you want it as fast as possible. One of the best ways to increase your wealth and put money in your pocket is by <u>Flipping</u> or rehabbing a house to quickly sell it. And rehabbing is the right term for some of these homes, often advertised as " Fixer Uppers"; Some are in desperate need of some TLC. Some are not. Just because a home may look hideous, does not exclude it from becoming a major money maker.

Fixer uppers can be found anywhere, in any neighborhood, in any city. Homes that may have been abandoned for whatever reason. This is where you can find great deals. This could be done by checking the newspaper, driving through your town, or word of mouth. Your local mailman of pizza delivery guy knows the city very well. I am sure he could tell you which streets have boarded up and abandoned homes. Ask them have they seen any homes that look abandoned, or as if they could use some fixing up; or tearing down. You could offer them money for any home that they have recommended and you buy. This will give them more of an incentive to help you and themselves.

Homes that are in this condition generally are undervalued. No one would expect to pay full price for a home that has had all the siding blown off and the roof gone. When looking for fixer uppers the same deal applies as before; do not limit yourself to searching for homes in a neighborhood that you would live in, or consider desirable. When you find yourself in an "undesirable area" what do you see? You see people living there. Some neighborhoods are perfect for some people and some are not. All you are concerned about is finding a great deal and leaving the property management and repair to the professionals. And remember you are not a professional property manager, you are a professional real estate investor. So do what you do best, invest. Maybe your buying and improving a home on a street may go so far as to improve the entire block.

When you find a home that needs fixing up, do not look at the home as being something that will not work for you just by looking at the damage that has been done to it. Do your homework. Look at the numbers. Find out how much the home would be worth if it was fully repaired. This is referred to as After Repair Value (ARV for short). How do you find that? You ask a real estate agent. Real Estate Agents can give you the after repair value of the home, and the prices of any similar homes in the area that have recently sold. The prices of the similar homes sold are referred to as <u>Comparables</u> (Comps as we in the business call them). After you have found the value, find out who the owner is (easy). The property owner's information can be found in any county or city in America. Most of the time on a county's website, you can find the homeowners information. Specifically, on the county auditor's website. Typically, that website will have the owner's name, address if different from the fixer upper's address, and the price that the owner paid for the home. Along with tax info, sale transaction history, and square footage.

An alternative way to contact the owner is to mail a letter to the address of the fixer upper. Address the letter to the name of the home owner or just put "Homeowner". Many times the home owner has the mail forwarded to his or her present address. You send them a letter stating that you want to buy the home, and that if they are interested in selling, to please give you a call. When they call, you tell them that you are a professional real estate investor and that you are interested in making an offer on their home. Ask how much they are asking for the home. Never ever, ever, open your mouth to let an offer come out before you have heard their asking price. You can always increase your offer. Very rarely can you take back an offer. More than likely, the homeowner will not tell you what offer he would have accepted. You will recognize whether or not it is a good deal by the amount of their asking price. As well as the amount of the comps that you received from the real estate agent. The farther apart the two numbers (comps and A.R.V.), the better. If you are wondering where to start your offers; I have always started my offers at 25% less than the asking price.

You are going to find some homes that are in squalled conditions. Why and how the house got in that condition is not a concern of yours at this point. All you care about are the numbers, and whether or not this deal will help you accomplish your goals. Your new buddy, the real estate agent, has informed you that the home has a value of $80000. Now, the owner tells you that he wants to sale the home for $20000. You think this is a great price, but what about all the repairs that are needed to get this house up and running? You attempt to negotiate with the owner until he tells you that he is not budging. So $20000 it is. A house that has damage and in need of repair for $20000, not a bad deal, right? You already know that if you get it fixed up, it would be worth $80000. So you agree to buy the house but you do not know how much it will cost to get this home repaired. You are not a professional home inspector, you are a professional real estate investor. So you tell the owner that you will buy the home for $20000 but you want to add in the contract/purchase agreement that you are to be given five days to get the home inspected. If you are not satisfied with the inspection you can back out of the deal. The owner agrees.

You must now contact another new friend of yours called the home inspector. You have to make sure he has experience and can give you some references of past satisfied customers, and copies of his work (photos, reports, etc). He must also be able to give you a cost range. A cost range will tell you how much it will cost you to get the home up and running. Make sure when interviewing home inspectors, that they have experience with investment and rehab properties. This is huge. Some inspectors are only experienced in working with new homes or homes in good, ready to move in condition.

The home inspector has done his job in three days. He has prepared a report for you with pictures, and has given you a report on every square inch of the property (roof, basement, yard, etc.). In the report he explains that the cost range is $10000 and $15000. Are you satisfied with that inspection? Be satisfied with the inspection before going forward.

You have determined that this is now a great deal for you. You call the seller and tell them that you are going forward on this deal. You now get the title work initiated, to search for any liens or mortgages on the property. When the title comes back clean (no liens, no mortgages), you then proceed to pay the seller.

Where do you come up with $20000 to pay the seller? You can pay him with the money that you accumulated from the deals you have done. You could use credit cards if you have high enough credit limits. Or you could use hard money loans. Hard moneys loans are short term loans made by private investors and lenders, who want a higher and faster return on their money. Hard money brokers have access to private lenders that want to loan you money at higher interest rates than they can receive from investing their money in stock or any other investment. You can borrow up to 55% to 65% of the after repair value. The interest rates on hard money loans are higher than normal loans, but they are often easier to get than traditional bank loans. And close faster. Most hard money lenders determine your eligibility not based on your credit, but on the deal that you were able to negotiate. For this deal, it would not be difficult to find a hard money lender. Hard Money lenders are listed on websites, newspaper classified sections, and your friend the mortgage broker may even have a few leads for you. In your purchase agreement, you have three to five days to have the home inspected. When the inspection comes back after three days, you now have two days to search for a hard money loan. They can qualify you and your deal in less than a day, and sometimes fund the deal in less than two weeks .

Now for the purposes of demonstration, I will show you how we are going to make this deal work. I am going to walk you through this deal step by step. It will serve as a reference example for you to come back to at a later date.

You have the purchase agreement written up for $20000. You have had the home inspected, and the cost range of repairs is $15000.

Purchase Price=$20000   After Repair Value=$80000
Repairs   =$15000
Total $35000

Now you have all the legalities, paperwork, and <u>due diligence</u> (title work, purchase agreement signed by you the buyer and the seller, and the inspection) is completed. You contact one of your new best friends, the hard money lender. You fill out their application and give them the info on the property. They will approve you in a day or less. You have been approved for a loan of $40000, with a four month repayment period. After the purchase has been made the money that you need for repairs will be delivered to you in <u>draws</u>. What that means is that the hard money lender will give you money only as the work on the home progresses. He will break it down into 25% increments. When 25% of the rehab work is done, 25% more of the repair money is delivered.

Are you a <u>general contractor</u>? No, you are a professional real estate investor, right? So how are you going to get this house rehabbed? You hire a general contractor. The general contractor will take care of all of the details of getting the home rehabbed and ready for occupancy. Just like with the inspector, you want to do your homework when selecting a general contractor. Ask to see some of their previous work, make sure they are licensed and bonded, and ask for references as well.

The general contractor tells you that the house can be up and running in about three weeks. Your next step is to hire a project manager. The project manager will be your ears and eyes on the work site. He will give you reports and update you on the progress of the rehab job. He will give you the progress on the work that has been done. And when 25% of the job is completed, you or the hard money lender will give him 25% more money for repairs. Remember, the lender is only going to give you money, in draws, and/or as the repairs are completed. You do not need to go to the home every other day to see if the work is being done. If you have a large number of deals going on at the same time and in different places, going to each site would be very time consuming. And also, you do not really know what you are looking at anyway. Unless you are a trained inspector, carpenter, painter, tradesperson, or skilled laborer, your presence is not necessary. You will more than likely just get in the way.

While the home is being repaired. You tell your friends that have been doing your property management, that you want to get a tenant in this home. But you are really interested in selling this home to get money in your pocket right away. A home already occupied with a tenant, is much more attractive to a potential investor than one that is unoccupied. The property management company tells you that you can get $800 per month in rent for that area. You say, "OK".

After some serious thinking, you have decided to sell the home, rather than hold it and rent it out. You have paid a total of $40000 for the home ($20000 for purchase + $15000 for repairs+ $5000 interest to the hard money lender). The interest paid is an estimate. Rates do vary depending upon the terms of the loan. The home is valued at $80000. You can place an ad in the newspaper, advertise it on the Internet, place a sign in the yard, or list it with a real estate agent. Or all of the above. Your asking price will determine how fast you sale the home. If you are willing to sale it quickly, you can take less profit and sale it at a lower price. Say, for instance, that you listed the house to sale for $65000. I think you would get offers on this home very, very quickly. If you sold the house for $65000, you would profit $25000 ($65000 - $40000). Not bad.

The repairs are complete. The house is up and running. It has made it out of rehab. You have a tenant ready to move in. You even have a buyer already lined up as well. What a great feeling. Everyone is happy. The new tenants will have a freshly rehabbed home to live in. The new buyer will have a newly rehabbed home and a new tenant with at least a one year lease. The hard money lender is happy and looking forward to doing business with you again. And you pocket at least $25000 on top of that. It took about three months for that one deal to pocket you $25000. How long would it take you to pocket $25000 in your current job? Now imagine doing two or three flips/ rehabs per month. Imagine that! It is achievable! Very Possible.

"Discontent is the first necessity of progress"
Thomas Edison

CHAPTER 6

Lease Options

The previous chapters covered just the basics in getting started on your way to riches in real estate. The previously written examples are just some of the ways that money is made. As you become a more experienced, professional real estate investor, you will begin to see things that maybe you might have over looked before. Small details that may have been overlooked that may have made you thousands more. You could adjust your formula to work as smoothly for you as possible. Every time.

There are numerous ways to do owner financing, rehabbing/fixer uppers, and ways to purchase a home for yourself. You may not want to flip or rent out every home that you come across. You may find your dream home using the exact same procedures that you used in searching for investment properties. One of techniques used to buy your primary home (a home that you plan to live in) is called lease optioning. Just as you used the lease option to obtain the home in chapter 4, you can also apply that formula for the purchase of your primary residence. You find a home that you would like to live in. It has a value of a little over $100,000. You contact the seller and see what the asking price is. Let us say that they tell you it is $100,000. You are not in a position to pay $100,000 in cash. Let us also say that you will not qualify for a bank loan. You offer them $91000. You explain to the seller what a lease option is, and ask if they would be interested. The seller tells you that they owe $80000 on the home, and that their monthly mortgage payments are $700 per month. And that they are very motivated to sell. "NO problem", you tell them. You say, "I will pay you $800 per month for the next five years. And I will give you a down payment of $5000 in cash." That offer allows the seller to pocket one hundred dollars per month over a five year period and put $5000 in her pocket. It sounds very attractive to the seller. You also agree to pay all property taxes, and insurance as well. This leaves the seller with no responsibility for the home. The payments will be paid to the title company. The title company will send the seller a check for $100 a month, and pay the sellers $700 mortgage to the bank. If you do not pay the seller, they can foreclose on the home and start their search for a new buyer. They also get to keep your $5000 down payment.

In the lease option contract you must include information which clearly states that $100 of the monthly payments, along with the $5000 go towards your down payment. So at the end of 5 years, you will have paid a total of $11000.

Now after five years, you have given the seller:
$6000 (monthly payments) +
$5000 (Initial Down Payment to the seller)=
$11000

A month or two prior to the end of the five year period, you call your buddy the mortgage broker and tell her to find you a loan and give her the details. You are buying the home for $91000, and you have already made a down payment of $11000. The mortgage broker easily finds a bank that will give you a home loan in the amount of $80000 ($91000 - $11000). Easily because you have vested $11000 into the property already.

Thus, you have received a bank loan for $80000. The sellers mortgage is paid in full. The seller pocketed $11000. You have a home that you have been living in for the past 5 years. Now the deed is in your name. Everyone is happy. Everybody wins.

The lease option is a great way to obtain a piece of property. It is a technique that does not require the need for you to have perfect credit. No bank application was filled out. Banks want to know your shoe size, what was for dinner last month, want bank statements from 1979, and a copy your high school lunch card. I am only kidding, but the home loan process is very tedious and exhausting. And it takes too much time. But it is a necessary evil. We need the banks to do their job of making sure that everything is legitimate and that all the I's are dotted and all of the T's are crossed.

That's why we as professional real estate investors have to really think outside of the box in order to find nontraditional ways to purchase real estate. You may never know what may or may not work unless you try it. You may come up with ideas or solutions that may seem outlandish, but you never know what a seller will accept as an offer. I have seen a seller accept a used pickup truck as a down payment. Use your brain (that big problem solver) and be creative.

I have shown you how I got in and out of the rat race. I have illustrated to you how investing in real estate is a way to make millions of dollars; if done correctly. I have included my mistakes and failures in hopes that you can learn from them. Use the formula that works. You have been given a formula that if applied as I stated, will work over and over again. There is no reason why you cannot do this. If I could get myself to a point in my life where I can do what I want to do, when I want to do it; you can too.

You have to have the will and the desire to change your life. All of the power that you need is right inside of you waiting for you to unleash it. Maybe you have other skills and talents that you have always wanted to showcase to the world. By investing in real estate, you can make enough money to be able to learn what it is you were put on this planet to do. It is hard to do that when you are on the clock and your manager or supervisor is on your back.

I have passed the formula on to you, as it was passed on to me. Use it to go. Use it and grow.

"Blessed is the person who perseveres under trial, because when she has stood the test, she will receive the crown of life that God has promised to those who love him."
-James 1:12

CHAPTER 7

Any Market

There are three basic needs: Shelter, Food, and Clothing. People are always going to need something to eat. One cannot survive without food. Daily tasks that require energy and brainpower cannot be completed unless one has received some form of nutrition.

Clothing is a necessary comfort that many in the industrialized nations of the World cannot go without. Although there are nudist colonies, the law states that a person must be properly clothed while in a public setting, less that person is deemed "Indecently" exposed. Also, in places where it snows, one would require several layers of clothing during the winter months, just to keep from freezing.

A roof over your head gives you a sense of security that cannot be substituted. "There is no place like home." I know many of you have heard that saying before. I am sure many have uttered that phrase. People are always going to need a place to live. As long as man has been on Earth, he has sought shelter. Shelter was and is still necessary to protect you from the elements and danger.

The World is getting smaller. Immigration continues to increase exponentially. The population in America is steadily increasing. As people begin to travel the World in search of a better life, they find themselves looking for that perfect place to call home. When a person makes the decision to move to a different city, or country for that matter, they must first find a place to live. Whether they consider renting or buying. Many look for condominiums, single family homes, and apartments. I know about this experience firsthand as I myself have relocated. When I decided to move, the first basic need I took care of was the need for shelter. Where was I going to live? I needed to find a place first before I set out on my journey. Even if that meant buying a home, leasing a condominium, or renting an apartment; I had to make a decision.

People will always need somewhere to live. No matter what the so called "experts" and "economists" report, people will continue to seek shelter. They will always need a place to call home. When the economy is so called "bad", do people automatically begin to sleep on the streets? No. When there is gloom and doom news of recessions and joblessness, do people still require roofs over their heads? Yes, they most certainly do.

It makes no difference what the Market is described as being or doing. There will always be a person looking to rent or buy a place to live. Take a look around you. Most of the people that you see at the grocery store, at the park, or in the airport have a place to live. Daily, many are looking for a new place to settle in and raise their families. Daily, thousands of people are searching the classified sections in search of a place to live. Where will they find it? Who will provide this potential renter or home buyer with their next home? Could it be you? You may be the person that made a decision to see the real picture and continue to invest in real estate no matter what the "Market" is reportedly doing. I find that I have been most successful when I run in the opposite direction from the crowd.

The news and supposed "experts" have painted a grim and dark picture of the real estate market. They have magnified the potential pitfalls and hazards of real estate investing during a time when there are an increasing number of foreclosures. What they fail to report is the fact that many of the foreclosures are a result of unscrupulous lenders who approved people for loans that they knew were predatory in nature, and with terms that the borrower could not reasonably afford to handle.

So to say that a specific time to invest in real estate is better than any other is false. The Market, the weather, if the ground hog sees its shadow on Ground Hog Day have nothing to do with whether or not you should invest in real estate. A deal is a deal. If you find a great home that is under priced, and you could rent that home out to a family and earn a couple hundred dollars per month profit; why would you pass that up just because of some supposed expert telling you that the real estate market is bad now? If you use the formulas that you have learned in this book, and have performed your due diligence, the reports regarding The Market do not matter. What only matters is whether or not it is a good deal or a bad deal.

Housing prices have increased since the 1900s. A house that was $30,000 in 1950 today is now worth 3 or 4 times as much. That's just the way that the economy and inflation works. The prices of things will continue to increase. The hot topic of today appears to be that the "Bubble" has burst. Meaning that home prices have reached their peaks, and will now begin to decrease in value. That the appraised values will be lower instead of higher. This information is important to a person that buys a home with intentions to sell it quickly for maximum profit; Flip It. But the person that invests for the long run, and wants to hold on to the property, can do a number of things with an investment property during times like these. If the Market is supposed to be so bad, you could buy a home and lease option it. Or you could just place the home up for rent. Holding on to a property could make you money no matter what else is going on in the economy. As long as the home is considered to be a good deal, you can make money during the roughest of times. By doing your due diligence, do not allow a good deal to pass you by.

So, regardless of what you have heard on television, from neighbors, on the Radio, and have read in the newspaper; it is never a bad time to invest in real estate. People need homes now and people will need homes in the future. You should question what the motives are behind this tidal wave of gloom that is being painted by the media regarding real estate. Across this country, more and more land is being cleared and developed right now for subdivisions with single family homes being built. What do those builders know that you don't? They know that people need shelter. Therefore, they may as well buy it, or rent it, or lease it from us! That should be your creed. Why not?

"Yesterday is gone. Tomorrow has not yet come. We have only today. Let us begin."
-Mother Teresa

CHAPTER 8

Giving Back

There are not many requirements of the wealthy other than this one: That you <u>Give Back</u>. And by giving back, I mean helping those that are less fortunate. By giving back, you are showing thanks to God by doing his work on Earth. God is not going to just pop up and start feeding the poor. God needs you to do that. God has chosen you to serve as his hands. You are now more equipped to do his work, more so now than ever before. It was hard to even think of doing charity work when you were broke.

By tithing, or donating to charities, or starting a scholarship or a foundation, God can work through you.

After you have taken care of your family, your next requirement is to care for your Worldly family. Have you ever wondered how people could give millions and millions of dollars to charities and foundations? They do it because they want to help mankind. The money is usually donated to schools, hospitals, and libraries. All are places that are designed to increase intelligence and life. By improving the world, you improve your own life. People that tithe and donate more, get more. It is a fact. Wealth is put in the hands of those that are going to do the most good with it. It is given to those that God can trust to do her will. Why should you be blessed with millions of dollars knowing that you are just going to horde it? Waste it on unnecessary things. Why do you think many people that win million dollar lotteries go through all of the money very quickly, and go right back to being broke? They never applied the principals of giving back. They just horde and overindulge; never taking time to show thanks by giving. As I mentioned before, those that will do the most good with money, will receive the most money, to do more good. That is a fact. Selfishness is sickness; a disease. That if left untreated, can spread poverty, bleakness, and gloom throughout the world. The only cure for such a disease is generosity and caring.

It is amazing how money, when placed in the right hands, can effect change. Money has been able to provide schools for little girls in South Africa; to provide them with a future that they could only have dreamed of. It is now becoming a reality. And for that I would like to say "Thank You, Oprah W."! Additionally, In the precise hands, money has been able to provide every student in an inner city school district with a personal computer in their home or school. For that I would like to also say" Thank You, Bill G."! Money has helped form foundations that have helped homeless individuals get off the street, find employment, and get a home. Thanks Angels! Benevolence has helped make advances in medicines and sciences, that could help improve and strengthen the lives of every human being on the planet.

Giving back is very important. It is very necessary. Pick

a cause or two, or three. There are millions of charities and foundations that could use your help. If you need any suggestions, contact your local church, synagogue, temple, mosque, recreation center, school, hunger center, homeless shelter, free clinic, or hospital. I am confident that someone there can help you. Just think; the money that you donate will have an everlasting effect on the lives of countless others. Now, and in the future.

The significance of tithing and donating can never be stressed enough. This book was designed to open your eyes to your present surroundings, and find the unlimited cash flow which you thought was out of your reach. When you begin to gain the prosperity that you want, you would like to be able to keep it. In order to keep the wealth stream flowing smoothly, you have to give.

I realize that I have said, "in order to get you must give." But do not give just to get. Give to be able to give more. Give as a means of making a difference. At the end of the day, you want to be able to lay on your nice, comfortable, $1000 mattress, and say, "I helped someone, today." Give for the sake of giving, not for the sake of getting. Faithfully as God has blessed you with life and abundance, you too have the capability to bless others. And once you give, you will be surprised when you see how much you will receive.

"Everybody has their own private Mount Everest they were put on this earth to climb. You may never reach the summit; for that you will be forgiven. But if don't make at least one serious attempt to get above the snow-line, years later you will find yourself lying on your deathbed, and all you will feel is emptiness"
-Hugh Macleod

CHAPTER **9**

Now Let's Go!

Months and months have passed. You have done many deals. You have accumulated all of this wealth, and now what do you do with it? Do you get a car? Buy a boat? Visit six continents in 7 weeks? Organize that foundation you have been thinking about? The answer is YES! We can now begin to see and enjoy life without having to worry about money. I have learned that you make your best decisions when you are happiest. Your vision is clearer. You can see the bigger picture. You have expanded your mind while experiencing new things, new cultures, and new worlds. After having obtained wealth, you will have begun to fill your brain with new memories that you have created for yourself and your family, from the new experiences that you have provided for them. Your family will thank you for all that you have done for them. Your friends will admire you as a success. More money will be attracted to you. People will want to know how you did it. You can show them by demonstration, or you can charge them a fee for consultation. My suggestion is that you tell them to buy this book called Stop! Now Let's Go! Either way, you get more money, more money, more! Nothing is wrong with more money. That is a good thing. The more you have, the more you can do. The more you have, the more you can help.

Through you, God can enjoy the beautiful vacations that you and your family have taken and will take. God can see a child's face light up after you have given them a gift. Through you, God can watch the reaction of that homeless man as you give him warm clothes or money to buy something to eat.

Believe it or not, you were chosen to read this book. By reading this book, you are acknowledging that you want more. You have taken a step towards improving your life and having more. By reading this book, you are taking a step towards improving your finances and getting closer to accomplishing all of your life's goals. Action is the number one thing that separates dreamers from doers. Dreamers dream all day long about having a big house and a big car, but never get off of the couch, for fear that they may miss the next top model or american idol. Some watch so many reality shows that they have forgotten what reality is. They call up other dreamers to make sure that they have not gotten up off of the sofa as well. Misery loves company.

If you have time to watch television all day long, you must be satisfied and content with your life. If you are not satisfied with your life, and you are watching hours and hours of television per week, what are you doing with your life? How are you helping your situation? If you are not living the life that you truly want, what are you waiting for to take action? I am puzzled at how so many can have time to watch hours and hours of television, and accomplish nothing. But claim to want a better life. I have met people that proclaim to want a better life, but rarely take one step towards accomplishing their goals. Some do not know how to get started. Many are not motivated. Whatever the reason, the bottom line is this; they live their lives constantly complaining and blaming. And getting nowhere. No action, no satisfaction.

However, you have taken a step forward. By reading this book, you have taken action. Now apply what you have learned from this book and get the life that you want.

You have to See It, Believe It, Want It, Do It, and Get It!

Now let us stop daydreaming and start doing. Let's stop thinking small and start to think BIG! Let's stop being broke and go get your wealth. It is waiting for you. All you have to do is go get it. There is more than enough money to go around.

"There is money sitting in a bank somewhere, waiting for you to withdraw it".
-Marvin C. Hudson, Jr.

Now let's GO!

Here is what you need to do to get started:
- Obtain Credit report
- Obtain Credit score
- Apply for credit cards (apply for as many as you can find, online and paper applications)
- Gain access to a computer with Internet (Home or public library)
- Look for deals (newspaper, realtor, driving neighborhoods, and Internet)
- Make Offers!!!!!!!!!
- Locate real estate professionals in your area (Realtors, property management companies, property inspectors, general contractors, mortgage brokers, title companies, and hard money lender): Call them up, and ask them questions about what it is they do. There is no such thing as a dumb question. They will be more than happy to give you as much info as you need, in return for future business.

Glossary

Words, Terms, and Helpful Phrases

Acre
A quantity of land equal to 43,560 square feet.

Amortization
The reduction of debt over a fixed term on an installment basis.

Amortized Loan
A loan in which the principal as well as the interest is payable in monthly or other periodic installments over the term of the loan.

Appraisal
An estimation of value of real property at the present date.

Appraiser
A person with no interest in the property who evaluates a property and determines a value for it. Using the cost approach, income approach, and/or market data approach.

Appreciation
The growth in value of property.

Arrears
The payment of money after the fact. Monies owed that began to accumulate at a past time.

Assessed Value
The value placed on a property by the taxing department of a county or a tax assessor. This value is used for tax purposes.

Asset
Anything of value that may be used to make a payment or to trade.

Assign
To transfer ones right to purchase a property to another person.

Assume a mortgage
Usually under the discretion of the bank or lien holder, a person takes over the responsibility of making payments on a property.

Balloon payment
A large final payment due on a note, usually after smaller payments have been made.

Bankruptcy
Proceedings against a debtor, who has been declared legally insolvent, to distribute the debtor's property among the creditors.

Buyer's Broker
A broker who works on behalf of the buyer when entering a real estate transaction.

Cash Flow
Your gross income after all operating expenses and debt are paid for a particular property.

Closing Date
A predetermined date in which a real estate transaction will take place.

Contingency
A possible event based on the happening of an uncertain future event.

Contract
A legally binding agreement between two or more people which creates an agreement to do or not to do something.

Counter Offer
A change in price or terms of an unacceptable offer.

Deed
An instrument conveying title to, and ownership of real
    property. Deeds are recorded by county recorders and/
    or assessors.

Default
Failure to pay a loan or to fulfill a financial obligation.

Distressed Property
A property that has been priced well below its repaired val-
    ue. Distressed properties have been either abandoned,
    foreclosed on, or bank owned.

Earnest Money
Deposit money given to the seller from the buyer to bind
    the contract of purchase of property. The earnest mon-
    ey is generally credited towards the purchase price.

Equity
In real estate, the value of an interest a person holds over
    and above any mortgage or liens on the property.

Escape Clause
A clause added to a contract that allows either party the
    option of exiting or terminating the contract.

Escrow
Money held by a neutral party.

Fair Market Value
The value of a property in comparison to similar properties
    on the market.

Flipping a house
Buying a property with the intentions to sell it for a profit.

Flexible Seller
A seller who is very motivated to sell a property and is
    more than willing to use nontraditional means of get-
    ting their property sold.

Foreclosure
The process whereby property pledged as security on a
    note is sold under court order because of default on
    the note.

Interest Rate
An amount a borrower must repay in addition to the full
    amount of the loan.

Lease
A contractual agreement between a home or property own-
    er, and a tenant. The lease allows the tenant to reside in
    or on the property for a specified period of time.

Lease Option
An agreement between a property owner and a buyer,
    where the property owner agrees to sell the property
    to the buyer at a future date. The buyer lives in the
    property, or leases it until the lease option expires at a
    predetermined date.

Letter of Intent
A letter stating a buyer's intentions to make an offer to buy
    a property. It is not a legally binding document.

Lien

The right of a creditor to take and/or sell a property in the event of a default. The proceeds from the sell will satisfy the obligation of a debt.

Listing Broker

A broker or agent that has access to the MLS (Multiple Listing Service). This person will be able to provide you with a list of available properties, and place a property that you want sold on the MLS.

Mortgage

A note that is owed as a result of the purchase of a property through financing or by receiving a loan.

Multiple Listing Service

A multi-realty service whereby members of a local real estate board exchange their listings.

Negative Cash Flow

When a rental property does not produce enough income to cover the cost of ownership. The owner has to come out of pocket to cover the expenses.

No-Doc Loan

A loan where the lender does not require any documentation.

P.I.T.I

An abbreviation for Principal, Interest, Taxes, and Insurance.

Positive Cash Flow

When a rental property produces enough income, after expenses, to cover the cost of ownership. The owner is able to make a profit.

Title Search

A preliminary review of all previously recorded documents regarding a specific property. Provides a listing of liens and ownership of a property.

Promissory Note

A written document stating that a person owes another. It includes the amount owed, the date that it has to be paid, and the terms or payment.

Quit Claim Deed

A deed transferring whatever interest in the property, if any, that the grantor may have. They are usually used to clear title.

Realtor

A broker who is a member of the National Association of Realtors. Has access to the MSL. A professional with expertise in buying and selling property.

Security Deposit

An amount of money paid by a tenant before moving into a leased property. The security deposit is used to cover any damages incurred while living there, or to protect the landlord/owner in the event that the tenant moves out of the property prior to the end of the lease. Security deposits are usually refunded to the tenant if at the end of the lease, the tenant has caused no damage to the property and has been current with rent payments.

Tenant

A person having the temporary use and occupancy of a property owned by another person. The tenant usually pays rent at a rate agreed upon between them and the owner. And for a specified period of time.

Terms

The exact way that a property will be purchased.

Title Insurance

Insurance issued by a title company guaranteeing the title to be good and marketable.

Title Insurance Company

A business that reports on the status for the title on a specific property and whether or not it has any liens against it.

www.ingramcontent.com/pod-product-compliance
Lightning Source LLC
Chambersburg PA
CBHW022113170526
45157CB00004B/1607